WHY DO LOBSTERS EAT EACH OTHER?

AND OTHER ODD CRUSTACEAN ADAPTATIONS

BY THERESE SHEA

Gareth Stevens
PUBLISHING

Please visit our website, www.garethstevens.com. For a free color catalog of all our high-quality books, call toll free 1-800-542-2595 or fax 1-877-542-2596.

Library of Congress Cataloging-in-Publication Data

Names: Shea, Therese, author.
Title: Why do lobsters eat each other? : and other odd crustacean adaptations/ Therese Shea.
Description: New York : Gareth Stevens Publishing, [2019] | Series: Odd adaptations
Identifiers: LCCN 2017040805| ISBN 9781538220238 (library bound) | ISBN
9781538220252 (pbk.) | ISBN 9781538220269 (6 pack)
Subjects: LCSH: Crustacea–Adaptations–Juvenile literature. | Adaptation
(Biology)–Juvenile literature. | CYAC: Crustaceans.
Classification: LCC QL437.2 .S5425 2018 | DDC 595.3–dc23
LC record available at https://lccn.loc.gov/2017040805

First Edition

Published in 2019 by
Gareth Stevens Publishing
111 East 14th Street, Suite 349
New York, NY 10003

Copyright © 2019 Gareth Stevens Publishing

Designer: Sarah Liddell
Editor: Therese Shea

Photo credits: Cover, pp. 1, 17 ullstein bild/Contributor/ullstein bild/Getty Images; background used throughout Captblack76/Shutterstock.com; p. 4 Alexander Sviridov/Shutterstock.com; p. 5 (lobster) Chaiyaphuek Sooksupun/Shutterstock.com; p. 5 (shrimp) Sukpaiboonwat/Shutterstock.com; p. 6 Henry William Fu/Shutterstock.com; p. 7 Jeff Rotman/Photolibrary/Getty Images; p. 8 Simagart/Shutterstock.com; p. 9 Andrey Nekrasov/Getty Images; p. 10 Andrey Starostin/Shutterstock.com; p. 11 Scott Leslie/Minden Pictures/Minden Pictures/Getty Images; p. 12 SIMON SHIM/Shutterstock.com; p. 13 Hugh Lansdown/Shutterstock.com; p. 14 Richard Whitcombe/Shutterstock.com; p. 15 DEA PICTURE LIBRARY/Contributor/De Agostini/Getty Images; p. 16 Wolfgang Poelzer/WaterFrame/Getty Images; p. 18 Ennie/Shutterstock.com; p. 19 Fotosearch/Getty Images; p. 20 Dornicke/Wikimedia Commons; p. 21 Ayacop/Wikimedia Commons; pp. 22, 23 Ar rouz/Wikimedia Commons; p. 25 (top) Epipelagic/Wikimedia Commons; p. 25 (bottom) Roland Birke/Photographer's Choice/Getty Images; p. 26 Dante Fenolio/Science Source/Getty Images; p. 27 Danita Delimont/Gallo Images/Getty Images; p. 29 WoodysPhotos/Shuttterstock.com.

Printed in the United States of America

CPSIA compliance information: Batch #CS18GS: For further information contact Gareth Stevens, New York, New York at 1-800-542-2595.

CONTENTS

Curious About Crustaceans 4

Crazy Crabs 6

Lobster Cannibals! 10

Weird Woodlice 12

Menacing Mantis Shrimp .14

Strange Skeleton Shrimp .16

Bizarre Barnacles 18

Eerie Isopods 20

Odd Copepods 24

Unusual Ostracods 26

Crucial Crustaceans 28

Glossary 30

For More Information 31

Index 32

Words in the glossary appear in **bold** type the first time they are used in the text.

CURIOUS ABOUT CRUSTACEANS

THERE ARE MORE THAN 45,000 SPECIES, OR KINDS, OF CRUSTACEANS ON EARTH. Most live in water. Lobsters, crabs, and shrimp are crustaceans you know—and may have eaten! Crustaceans are named for their hard outer shell, called an exoskeleton. They usually have two pairs of antennae and a pair of body parts near the mouth called mandibles that work like jaws. Most use gills to breathe and have several pairs of legs for walking or swimming.

But many crustaceans have **evolved** different bodies as well as different ways of life to better suit their **habitats**. Some have adaptations that are really quite odd!

ALL ARTHROPODS

Crustaceans are arthropods. All arthropods are invertebrates, which means they have no backbone. They have an exoskeleton, a sectioned body, many pairs of limbs, and jointed legs. Other kinds of arthropods are insects and arachnids, the animal group that includes spiders. **SCIENTISTS THINK THAT ALL ARTHROPODS EVOLVED FROM ONE COMMON ANCESTOR!**

CRAB

COMMON FEATURES OF A CRUSTACEAN

FREE-SWIMMING LARVAE WITH SIMPLE, UNSEGMENTED BODY

GILLS FOR BREATHING

EXOSKELETON WITH A CARAPACE, OR A HARD SHELL ON ITS BACK

LEGS WITH JOINTS

MANDIBLES USED AS JAWS

THREE-PART BODY MADE UP OF HEAD, THORAX (MIDDLE), AND ABDOMEN (STOMACH)

EYES ON RAISED STALKS

MANY PAIRS OF LIMBS

THE WORD "CRUSTACEAN" COMES FROM THE LATIN WORD *CRUSTA*, WHICH MEANS "SHELL."

LOBSTER

SHRIMP

CRAZY CRABS

The largest and most numerous crustacean group is the decapods. Decapods include the giant Japanese spider crab, which has legs that stretch up to 12 feet (3.7 m)! This crab has some odder adaptations, too. **IT PICKS UP SEA ANIMALS SUCH AS SPONGES AND SEA ANEMONES AND STICKS THEM TO ITS SHELL.** It does this to make its own **camouflage** to hide from predators!

When predators such as octopuses attack the giant Japanese spider crab, the crustacean might leave one, two, or even three of its legs behind and still survive. It can grow these legs back when it molts!

MOLTED CRAB
EXOSKELETON

MORE ABOUT MOLTING

The exoskeleton is an adaptation that protects the soft body beneath, keeps it from becoming dry, and provides a place for muscles to attach. **CRUSTACEANS MOLT, OR CAST OFF, THEIR EXOSKELETONS AS THEY GROW.** The old exoskeleton separates from the body. The new exoskeleton forms beneath. The old exoskeleton then splits and is left behind.

WHEN GIANT JAPANESE
SPIDER CRABS ARE LARVAE,
THEY'RE SMALL AND ROUND.
THEY DON'T HAVE LEGS AT ALL.
THEIR LEGS GROW THROUGHOUT
THE REST OF THEIR LIFE.

The hairy crab, sometimes also called the teddy bear crab, can be found in the Red Sea and the Indian and the Pacific Oceans, especially near Australia and Japan. Hairy crabs are usually between 1 and 2 inches (2.5 and 5 cm) in length.

Hairy crabs have long hairs called setae all over their body. This adaptation protects the crab from predators. It's a kind of camouflage on rocky reefs, and it makes the outline of the crab's body hard to see. **THE SETAE ALSO TRAP BITS OF DIRT AND DEBRIS FLOATING BY, WHICH HELPS THE HAIRY CRAB TO BLEND IN EVEN MORE!**

COOPERATING CREATURES

The pom-pom crab is found in warm waters of the Indian and the Pacific Oceans. It has a symbiotic relationship with sea anemones, which means the animals help each other. **THE CRAB HOLDS AN ANEMONE IN EACH CLAW AND USES THEM TO STING PREY.** The anemone, in return, travels to new places and new food sources with the crab.

POM-POM CRAB

HAIRY CRABS EAT MOSTLY ALGAE.

LOBSTER CANNIBALS!

The decapods called lobsters are known for their large claws. These help them fight predators, such as cod, as well as catch prey, such as clams and crabs—and other lobsters. **YES, LOBSTERS ARE CANNIBALS, WHICH MEANS THEY EAT THEIR OWN SPECIES!**

This behavior has been growing more common in recent years. Scientists blame it on several factors. First, water temperatures are rising all over the world. This makes lobsters grow faster and reproduce more often. Second, overfishing has robbed oceans of lobsters' predators and prey. So, there are a lot more lobsters in the ocean with less to eat!

A LOOK INSIDE A LOBSTER

Don't look for a lobster's teeth in its mouth. **ITS TEETH ARE IN ITS STOMACH!** When a lobster eats, the food is ground up in the stomach by three teethlike body parts. These are called the "gastric mill." The American lobster has three stomachs in all—and can weigh up to 44 pounds (20 kg)!

10

AMERICAN LOBSTER

THE LARGER CLAW OF A LOBSTER—THE CRUSHER CLAW—CAN EASILY BREAK A CLAMSHELL. THE OTHER—THE RIPPER CLAW—IS USED FOR TEARING UP SOFTER FOOD, SUCH AS WORMS.

CRUSHER CLAW

RIPPER CLAW

WEIRD WOODLICE

Crustaceans call many kinds of habitats home, including oceans, seas, lakes, and rivers. They live in freshwater, salt water, and brackish waters, which are a mix of freshwater and salt water. Crustaceans can be found from the Arctic to the Antarctic.

SOME CRUSTACEANS ARE AMPHIBIOUS, WHICH MEANS THEY CAN LIVE ON LAND AND IN WATER. These include woodlice. In fact, the woodlouse can be found in nearly every habitat in the world except polar areas and dry deserts. There are about 3,500 species. Woodlice curl up into a ball to protect themselves from predators such as centipedes, spiders, and wasps.

WHAT'S FOR DINNER, WOODLOUSE?

Woodlice eat dead plants and fungi, which makes them an important part of their food web. **THEY ALSO EAT THEIR OWN POOP, BUT THEY DON'T PEE!** What a weird adaptation! Woodlice get rid of waste by making a strong-smelling chemical called ammonia, which passes out of their shell as a gas.

A WOODLOUSE HAS TWO SMALL "TUBES" CALLED UROPODS STICKING OUT OF ITS BACK. THEY HELP IT FIND ITS WAY. SOME SPECIES USE UROPODS TO GIVE OFF CHEMICALS THAT KEEP PREDATORS AWAY.

MENACING MANTIS SHRIMP

The colorful mantis shrimp is mostly famous for its claws, which are truly weapons. There are more than 350 species of mantis shrimp. Some use their claws to smash through the hard shells of clams and snails. Others use them to jab fish and other tasty sea animals with soft bodies, such as worms. **MANTIS SHRIMP ATTACK THEIR PREY ABOUT 50 TIMES FASTER THAN YOU CAN BLINK YOUR EYES!**

A mantis shrimp's punch is so powerful that it isn't found in many aquariums. **IT CAN PUNCH THROUGH THE WALLS OF A GLASS TANK!** Mantis shrimp also need to be kept separate so they don't kill other creatures.

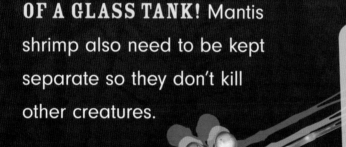

NOT A TRUE SHRIMP

Mantis shrimp aren't the same as the shrimp you eat, which belong in the decapod group with crabs, lobsters, and crayfish. However, they look similar. Mantis shrimp are a kind of crustacean called a stomatopod. Besides their weapon-like claws, stomatopods are known for the interesting tail fan on the rear of their body.

MORE FUN
MANTIS SHRIMP FACTS

GROANS TO ATTRACT
MATES AND WARN OTHERS
TO STAY AWAY

MAY SEAL THE OPENING
OF ITS DEN WITH MUCUS

CAN SEE MORE COLORS
AND KINDS OF LIGHT
THAN ANY OTHER ANIMAL

CREATES BUBBLES
WHEN IT MOVES THAT
CAN KNOCK OUT PREY

CAN "HEAR" WITH TINY
HAIRS ON ITS BODY

CAN KICK ITS FEET
AT SPEEDS OF
ABOUT 75 FEET (23 M)
PER SECOND

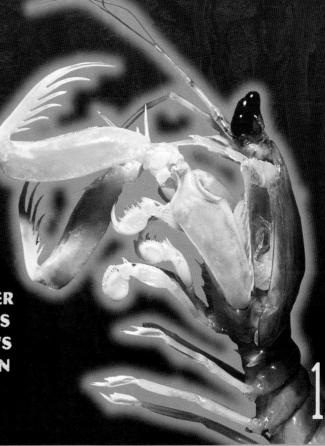

EACH EYE IS LARGER
THAN ITS BRAIN

SOME PEOPLE CALL THE MANTIS
SHRIMP "THUMB SPLITTERS" AFTER
EXPERIENCING THE CRUSTACEAN'S
FAMOUS CLAWS! WHEN THE CLAWS
AREN'T IN USE, THEY'RE TUCKED IN
UNDER THE SHRIMP'S HEAD.

STRANGE SKELETON SHRIMP

Skeleton shrimp are tiny, see-through crustaceans that belong to a group called amphipods. Skeleton shrimp have hooked back legs that allow them to hold onto underwater surfaces, keeping still until prey such as worms come by. Their shape and color, often brown or green, help them blend into their background. Some species can change color, too.

SKELETON SHRIMP POPULATIONS CAN GROW SO LARGE IN SOME PLACES THAT THEY APPEAR TO COVER SURFACES LIKE A RUG! This is bad news for fish, as the amphipods eat up the food sources they share, such as **plankton**. They also eat baby fish, called fry.

PRAYING MANTISES OF THE SEA

A skeleton shrimp's front legs look a bit like a praying mantis's. Also like praying mantises, mates sometimes kill each other. Males often fight each other for the chance to mate with a female. AFTER MATING, THE FEMALE SKELETON SHRIMP OF SOME SPECIES POISON AND EAT THE MALES!

SKELETON SHRIMP USUALLY AREN'T ANY LONGER THAN 2 INCHES (5 CM). THEY LIVE IN SALT WATER NEAR COASTAL AREAS.

BIZARRE BARNACLES

BARNACLES HAVE ONE OF THE ODDEST ADAPTATIONS OF ALL—THEY DON'T MOVE! There are more than 1,000 kinds. They're found on rocks, wood, seaweed, and the bodies of animals such as whales.

Young barnacles can swim. When they settle on a surface, they use a kind of cement to fix themselves in place. **IT'S AMONG THE MOST POWERFUL GLUES IN THE WORLD!** Then, the creatures build their hard outer shell.

Barnacles can still reproduce, even though they don't move. A barnacle **fertilizes** its neighbor's eggs by extending a special tube. **MOST BARNACLES HAVE BOTH MALE AND FEMALE REPRODUCTIVE ORGANS!**

GOOSE BARNACLES

PARASITES!

About 260 species of barnacles live within crabs and other crustaceans! For instance, the barnacle called *S. carcini* can grow throughout a green crab's body. It's called a parasite because it feeds on the **nutrients** the crab takes in. It makes the crab into a kind of zombie that cares for the parasite's eggs!

19

EERIE ISOPODS

Isopods are a group of crustaceans that has over 10,000 species! Some live in salt water, others in freshwater, and still others live on land. Most have a long, flat body with a back covered by wide plates. They usually have six pairs of limbs, but sometimes as few as two or as many as eight.

Most isopods are very small—some as small as 0.028 inch (0.7 mm) long. "Giant" isopods such as *Bathynomus giganteus* grow as large as 14 inches (36 cm) long. ONE *BATHYNOMUS GIGANTEUS* FOUND ATTACHED TO AN UNDERWATER ROBOT WAS 2.5 FEET (76 CM) LONG!

SCIENTISTS THINK *BATHYNOMUS GIGANTEUS* MAY HAVE ADAPTED TO GROW SO LARGE TO WITHSTAND THE GREAT PRESSURE ON ITS BODY IN THE DEEP OCEAN.

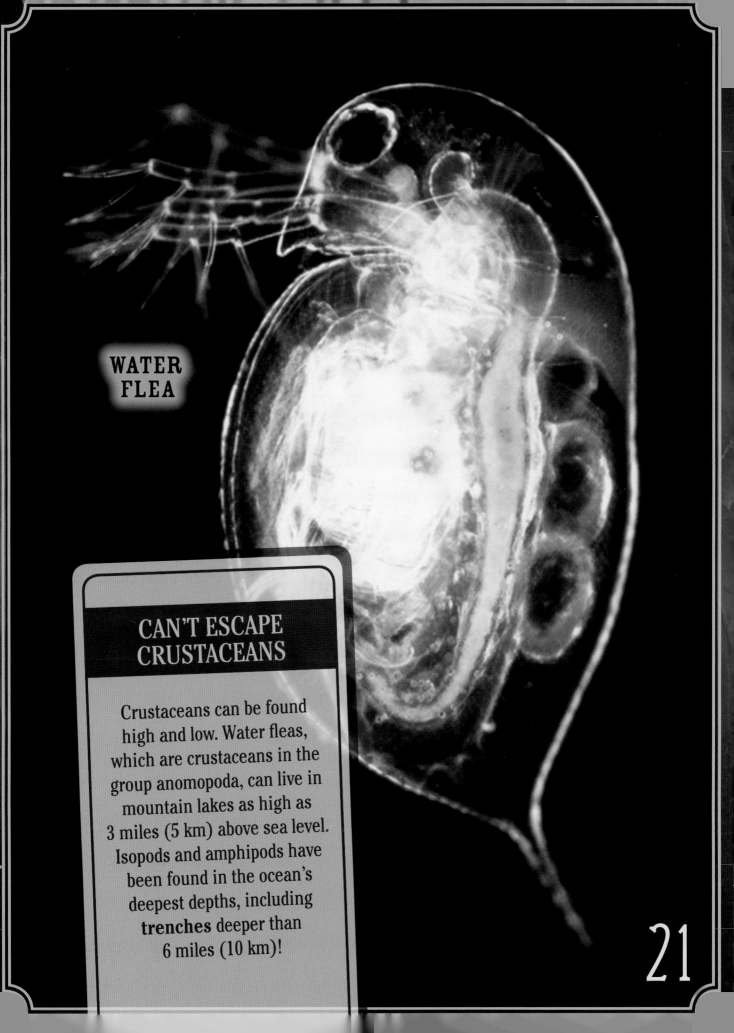

WATER
FLEA

CAN'T ESCAPE
CRUSTACEANS

Crustaceans can be found
high and low. Water fleas,
which are crustaceans in the
group anomopoda, can live in
mountain lakes as high as
3 miles (5 km) above sea level.
Isopods and amphipods have
been found in the ocean's
deepest depths, including
trenches deeper than
6 miles (10 km)!

Gribbles are water-dwelling isopods that look a bit like woodlice. There are about 20 species. **THESE CRUSTACEANS HAVE A STRANGE DIET—THEY EAT WOOD THAT'S FOUND IN WATER.** This might include trees swept into the sea, docks, sunken boats—or perfectly seaworthy boats!

Gribbles have a body with 14 segments, but can be as small as 0.04 inch (1 mm). That makes them hard to spot under the surface of ships. People who own wooden boats have to be careful to paint the bottom so gribbles won't tunnel in and make themselves at home.

EVOLVING AN ENZYME

Scientists are studying gribbles, hoping these animals might be able to turn plant waste into fuel people can use. Gribbles have evolved to be able to make an **enzyme** called cellulase that breaks down plant cell walls. **THIS MEANS GRIBBLES COULD HELP US TURN PAPER AND WOOD WASTE INTO LIQUID FUEL!**

HOLES IN WOOD MADE BY GRIBBLES

GRIBBLES ARE USUALLY A
YELLOW, WHITE, OR GRAY COLOR.

ODD COPEPODS

Copepods are another kind of crustacean. There are over 13,000 species, providing an important food source for other sea creatures. Unlike most crustaceans, copepods lack a carapace, which is the plate over the back that looks like a shield.

The copepod called the sea sapphire is usually see-through. **HOWEVER, MALE SEA SAPPHIRES SHINE WITH BEAUTIFUL COLORS WHEN THEIR BODY CAPTURES LIGHT.** Scientists think this adaptation may serve to catch the attention of a female in order to mate. When male sea sapphires aren't shining in the light, they seem to disappear—a great trick to avoid predators!

JUST ONE PARENT NEEDED

Most copepods need to mate in order to reproduce. **HOWEVER, CERTAIN SPECIES REPRODUCE BY A PROCESS CALLED PARTHENOGENESIS. THAT MEANS EGGS GROW INTO NEW INDIVIDUALS WITHOUT BEING FERTILIZED BY A MALE.** The advantage of this adaptation is that females don't have to find a male in order to keep the species going!

MOST COPEPODS GROW TO
BE LESS THAN 0.08 INCH
(2 MM) LONG. MOST SPECIES
LIVE IN FRESHWATER, BUT
SOME PREFER SALT WATER.

UNUSUAL OSTRACODS

There are about 8,000 species of crustaceans in the group called ostracods. They range in size from 0.004 to 1.3 inches (0.1 to 33 mm). The giant ostracod, or *Gigantocypris agassizii*, is larger than other ostracods, but is usually no bigger than a grape! Most ostracods are found on the bottom of oceans or lakes. Others live on land in wet places such as within mosses.

AN OSTRACOD'S BODY ISN'T MUCH MORE THAN A HEAD! Since they look like a shrimp inside a seedpod, they're sometimes called seed shrimp. Because of their pod, people sometimes mistake ostracods for tiny clams or mussels.

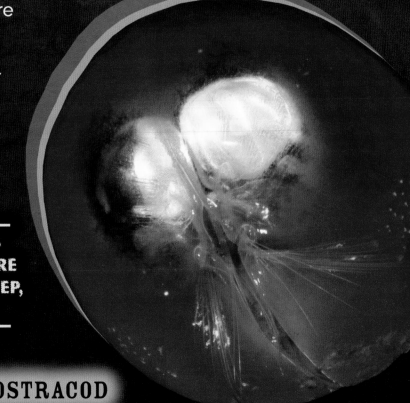

THE GIANT OSTRACOD HAS LARGE YELLOW EYES THAT ARE ADAPTED TO FIND PREY IN DEEP, DARK OCEAN WATERS.

GIANT OSTRACOD

26

AWESOME ANTENNAE

An ostracod usually has four or five pairs of limbs on its head. However, it can tuck itself into its pod so only its antennae show. When the pod is open, the antennae are used to move, feel, and feed. **THE GIANT OSTRACOD SWIMS BY ROWING ITS ANTENNAE LIKE OARS!**

OSTRACODS ON
A SEA CUCUMBER

27

CRUCIAL CRUSTACEANS

There are many, many more kinds of crustaceans. They have all kinds of adaptations, some odd but all extraordinary. And it's a good thing they have these to survive in their habitats because crustaceans are essential to their food webs. Without them, countless animals would go hungry.

For example, the tiny crustaceans called krill are a large part of the diet of whales. **OTHER CRUSTACEANS ARE HELPFUL FOR RECYCLING NUTRIENTS IN THE BODIES OF DEAD ORGANISMS.** Crustaceans are also a part of people's diets and fishing economies worldwide. Crustaceans are truly important creatures, whether they're on land or in the water!

CRUSTACEANS IN CRISIS

IN RECENT YEARS, MANY SCIENTISTS HAVE BECOME CONCERNED ABOUT THE GROWING ACIDITY OF THE WORLD'S OCEANS. They blame this on increased amounts of carbon dioxide on Earth, likely because of the burning of **fossil fuels**. This has an alarming effect on crustaceans. IT MAKES IT HARDER FOR THEM TO FORM THEIR PROTECTIVE EXOSKELETONS.

IN 2015 ALONE, FISHING PRODUCED $208 BILLION IN SALES IN THE UNITED STATES!

GLOSSARY

ancestor: an animal in the past from which a modern animal evolved

camouflage: something, such as color or shape, that protects an animal from attack by making the animal hard to see in the area around it

debris: pieces that are left after something has been broken or destroyed

enzyme: chemical matter in animals and plants that helps to cause natural processes

evolve: to change slowly, often into a better or more advanced state

fertilize: to make an egg able to grow

fossil fuel: a fuel such as coal, oil, or natural gas that is formed in Earth from dead plants or animals

habitat: the place or type of place where a plant or animal naturally or normally lives or grows

mucus: a thick liquid that is produced in some parts of the body, such as the nose

nutrient: something that plants, animals, and people need to live and grow

plankton: very small plant and animal life in an ocean or other body of water

sea anemone: a small, brightly colored sea animal that looks like a flower and sticks to rocks, coral, or other surfaces

trench: a long, narrow channel in the ocean floor

FOR MORE INFORMATION

BOOKS

Kalman, Bobbie. *Animals Without Backbones*. New York, NY: Crabtree Publishing, 2009.

Moore, Heidi. *Giant Isopods and Other Crafty Crustaceans*. Chicago, IL: Raintree, 2012.

Rustad, Martha E. H. *Lobsters*. Minneapolis, MN: Bellwether Media, 2008.

WEBSITES

The Arthropod Story
evolution.berkeley.edu/evolibrary/article/arthropodstory
Learn about the evolution of arthropods.

Crustaceans, Lobsters, Crabs and More
easyscienceforkids.com/all-about-crustaceans/
Read more about these invertebrates.

INDEX

amphipods 16, 21

anomopoda 21

antennae 4, 27

arthropods 4

barnacles 18, 19

camouflage 6, 8

cannibals 10

carapace 5, 24

cellulase 22

claws 8, 10, 11, 14, 15

copepods 24, 25

crabs 4, 6, 7, 8, 9, 10, 14, 19

decapods 6, 10, 14

exoskeleton 4, 5, 6, 28

fishing 10, 28, 29

food web 12, 28

fossil fuels 28

gills 4, 5

gribbles 22, 23

isopods 20, 21, 22

larvae 5, 7

limbs 4, 5, 6, 7, 16, 17, 20, 27

lobsters 4, 5, 10, 11, 14

mandibles 4, 5

molt 6

nutrients 19, 28

oceans 8, 10, 12, 21, 26, 28

ostracods 26, 27

parasite 19

plankton 16, 19

predators 6, 8, 10, 12, 13, 24

prey 8, 10, 14, 15, 16, 26

reproduction 10, 15, 17, 18, 24

setae 8

shell 4, 5, 6, 11, 12, 14, 18

shrimp 4, 5, 14, 15, 16, 17, 26

stomatopods 14

uropods 13

water fleas 21

woodlice 12, 13, 22